Cambridge Elements

Elements in Public and Nonprofit Administration
edited by
Andrew Whitford
University of Georgia
Robert Christensen
Brigham Young University

PARTNERSHIPS THAT LAST

Identifying the Keys to Resilient Collaboration

Heather Getha-Taylor
University of Kansas

CAMBRIDGE
UNIVERSITY PRESS

University Printing House, Cambridge CB2 8BS, United Kingdom

One Liberty Plaza, 20th Floor, New York, NY 10006, USA

477 Williamstown Road, Port Melbourne, VIC 3207, Australia

314–321, 3rd Floor, Plot 3, Splendor Forum, Jasola District Centre, New Delhi – 110025, India

79 Anson Road, #06–04/06, Singapore 079906

Cambridge University Press is part of the University of Cambridge.

It furthers the University's mission by disseminating knowledge in the pursuit of education, learning, and research at the highest international levels of excellence.

www.cambridge.org
Information on this title: www.cambridge.org/9781108745284
DOI: 10.1017/9781108775335

First published 2019

A catalogue record for this publication is available from the British Library.

ISBN 978-1-108-74528-4 Paperback
ISSN 2515-4303 (online)
ISSN 2515-429X (print)

Partnerships that Last

Identifying the Keys to Resilient Collaboration

Elements in Public and Nonprofit Administration

DOI: 10.1017/9781108775335
First published online: November 2019

Heather Getha-Taylor
University of Kansas
Author for correspondence: hgtaylor@ku.edu

Abstract: Communities across the United States face a variety of vexing and intractable problems that are not easily – or quickly – solved by any one organization or sector. Rather, partners must work together over time to address these shared priorities. It also requires an individual and collective ability to overcome the challenges and setbacks that arise along the way. A key question emerges: *what keeps community partnerships strong over time?* This Element compares and contrasts a sample of enduring voluntary partnerships with those that have ended to identify the features that contribute to *collaborative resilience*, or the ability of partnerships to respond productively to shocks and change over time.

Keywords: collaboration, resilience, community partnerships, critical junctures

ISBNs: 9781108745284 (PB), 9781108775335 (OC)
ISSNs: 2515-4303 (online), ISSN 2515-429X (print)

Contents

1 Introduction

While it can be said that working together is a strategy long adopted by communities to address collective needs (Blackmar, Getha-Taylor, Moen, & Pierce, 2018; O'Toole, 2014), it is also true that the imperative for collaboration gained traction in public and nonprofit management scholarship and practice in recent years. For example, Milward and Provan (2000) highlighted the considerable impact of contracting out on human services delivery. The authors' focus on the growing "hollow state" signaled a significant change in the public problem-solving approach. Similarly, Kettl (2002) argued that society's contemporary boundary-spanning issues did not fit the command-and-control assumptions of the bureaucratic structures that characterized traditional government responses. Collaboration and coordination, rather than authority and hierarchy, would be necessary to address twenty-first-century dilemmas.

These observations have proven accurate. Bungled cross-sector responses to disasters such as hurricanes Katrina and Rita in 2005, for example, sharply illustrated the essential nature of effective collaboration (Hicklin, O'Toole, Meier, & Robinson, 2009). Disasters are not the only context where boundary-spanning work is needed, of course. Whenever there are community issues that occur frequently, have lasting duration, affect many people, are disruptive to personal or community life, and are perceived as problems, the solutions will often require the input and resources of many partners (Community Tool Box, 2018). Examples of such issues include: homelessness eradication, pollution reduction, domestic violence reduction, ensuring humane treatment of animals, improved health outcomes, neighborhood revitalization, community education, youth development, and gang prevention.

These and other contemporary governance concerns indicate that the focus on collaboration is not a passing fad. Instead, the imperative to work together seems to grow stronger each year. For example, in response to the city's changing demographics, Aurora, Colorado, saw a need to institutionalize collaboration four years ago to effectively meet the needs of incoming immigrants and refugees (ICMA, 2019). Also, two years ago, Philadelphia institutionalized a collaborative approach to "smart city" design to "understand and implement smart and emerging technology solutions that would improve City service delivery for its broad community of residents, businesses, and visitors" (City of Philadelphia, 2019, p. 2). Further, collaboration has recently been identified the critical mechanism for addressing such entrenched and complex issues as the distrust that can exist between police and the communities they serve (Hillard Heintze, 2018). Finally, groups such as the Water Research

Foundation advocate for much broader and deeper collaboration in the future to ensure effective stewardship of our limited natural resources (Stoker, Pivo, & Howe et al., 2018).

Communities across the United States share these and other boundary-spanning public concerns. The forces driving the need for collaboration, including changing public service demands, resource limitations, ongoing privatization, and "wicked problems," span jurisdictions (Koliba, Meek, Zia, & Mills, 2018). As practitioners grapple with the increased need for effective collaboration, scholars also wrestle with this topic. Over the years, scholars developed a stream of competing definitions to represent its many facets (O'Leary & Viz, 2012). For the purposes of this project, Bryson, Crosby, and Stone's (2006) definition of collaboration is adopted: it is the linking or sharing of information, resources, activities, and capabilities to achieve an outcome that could not be achieved by organizations working separately.

While there is no shortage of definitions or studies on collaboration, this project is unique in its response to several gaps in the literature. First, *our collective understanding of collaboration lacks long-term focus.* In their review of cross-sector collaboration studies, Bryson, Crosby, and Stone (2015) noted the proliferation of single-case studies to the exclusion of longitudinal ones. The latter, they say, can offer a richer understanding of the complexities of collaboration and thus are needed. Similarly, in their comprehensive review of what is known about nonprofit collaboration to date, Gazley and Guo (2017) noted an imbalance in research, especially regarding our understanding of how collaborations evolve over time. To address the long-term problems mentioned, committed and lasting collaboration is needed. Understanding the elements that contribute to such resiliency and success over time is essential.

Related to this point, a second gap emerges: *the elements that are expected to lead to collaborative success are largely untested.* Some of the most prominent theories that serve to explain successful community-level collaboration, including theories of collaborative advantage (Huxham & Vangen, 2005), network life cycle (Lowndes & Skelcher, 1998), and adaptive capacity (Strichman, Bickel, & Marshood, 2008), are practically grounded, but the broader generalizability of these contributions is not well established. For this reason, this study applies these theories to a diverse sample of *community collaboratives.* According to Nowell (2009), community collaboratives are connected via voluntary ties rather than contractual arrangements. Their members work through informal relationships that make use of each member's expertise and resources. In addition, members of community collaboratives exercise some degree of autonomy when working together. These specific characteristics – voluntary ties, informal relationships, and member autonomy – provide an opportunity to examine what keeps community collaborations strong over time.

Third, *the multilevel elements of collaboration are not consistently captured in the literature*. While a multitude of studies have effectively examined collaboration at the organizational and interorganizational levels, other elements have received comparatively less attention. For example, one of the weaknesses in conceptualizations of collaborative governance is the failure to focus on individual actors (Kapacu, Hu, & Khosa, 2017; Torfing, 2016). Keast and Mandell's 2014 study illustrates an exception. In their review of Australian cross-sector collaborations, these authors identified three essential elements: 1) governance, management, and leadership; 2) collaborative systems/processes; and 3) individual competencies. However, even this comprehensive study did not consider some of the broader, external, and systemic features that impact internal collaborative dynamics (see Emerson & Nabatchi, 2015). This study builds upon these foundations and considers systemic, collaborative, and individual levels of community collaborations, which together contribute to their success or failure over time.

Fourth, *studies of cross-sector collaboration are not consistently balanced in their treatment of the diverse partners involved*. Even some of the most inclusive treatments of horizontal, or community-level, collaboration focus primarily on building capacity in government organizations (see Agranoff & McGuire, 2004; Forrer, Kee, & Boyer, 2014). This study offers an opportunity to consider the perspectives of other essential community partners who are necessarily involved in addressing vexing societal priorities. Namely, this study focuses on partnerships that include nonprofit collaborators that are often neglected in empirical studies (Cornforth, Hayes, & Vangen, 2015; Mitchell, O'Leary, & Gerard, 2015).

This project addresses these gaps by examining nineteen voluntary collaborations that each worked (or continue to work) on long-term, and generally intractable, community issues. The study sample is taken from the Foundation Center's Collaboration Hub database. Created in 2009, the database features descriptions of notable partnerships. The entries were solicited and reviewed for the Center's collaboration prize. The Center issued another call for submissions in 2011. These publicly available records now provide a snapshot of collaborations in time and also an opportunity to consider how those efforts have fared since then. This is accomplished via interviews with representatives of the collaborations in the sample and the use of critical juncture methodology. This methodological approach examines pivotal moments in time and the strategies used in those moments that determine future trajectories (Capoccia & Kelemen, 2007).

By comparing and contrasting accounts from collaboratives that have endured with those that have ended, this project seeks to identify the features that contribute to *collaborative resilience*. Resilience has been defined as "the ability of systems to cope with shocks and bounce back" (Black & Hughes, 2001, p. 16). It can apply to individuals, groups, organizations, and systems that respond productively to significant disruptive change (Witmer & Mellinger, 2016). Resilience is of particular interest given the community issues that the collaborations in this sample are working to address. While it might be expected that partnerships will end once their purpose is achieved, this study focuses on collaborations that exist to address long-term community issues that are not easily or quickly solved. As discussed by Quick and Feldman (2014, p. 674), while the concept of resilience has often been applied to organizations recovering from "acute crises," collaborative resilience allows systems and partners to continue to work together on shared goals over time despite disruptions. This study seeks to explore and elaborate the features that define this concept.

This study is unique in its long-term perspective, its use of critical juncture methodology to empirically examine factors for success, its multilevel focus including the systemic, collaborative, and individual features of resilience, and its consideration of diverse partners involved in community collaborations. Given these contributions, it is expected that findings from this study will offer value for collaboration scholars and students as well as for practitioners engaged in the challenging and important work of community partnerships.

2 Theoretical Foundations

Three theoretical lenses apply to this study. First, the theory of *collaborative advantage* grounds the effort's methodological approach and serves as the foundation for its core research question: *what differentiates partnerships that last over time?* Second, *life cycle* theory is used to explain the study's underlying evolutionary premise: that is, collaboratives can grow, change, adapt, and/or die. The study's third theoretical foundation, *adaptive capacity*, frames the study's goal of exploring and explaining collaborative resilience over time. Each theoretical lens is presented in the following sections.

2.1 Collaborative Advantage

Huxham and Vangen's (2005) theory indicates that, to gain advantage from collaboration, something has to be achieved collectively that could not have been achieved by any one of the organizations acting alone. This theory is aligned with Bryson, Crosby, and Stone's (2006) definition of collaboration that guides this research. Huxham and Vangen's collaborative advantage theory also captures the idea of *collaborative inertia*, or the phenomenon that occurs when some collaborations make slow progress and others die without achieving anything. This concept is of special interest to this study. Specifically, it is a goal of this work to answer the question: *what differentiates collaborative outcomes over time?*

In addition to utilizing this theory as a guide for the core research question, the present study also utilizes a sampling approach that is similar to Huxham and Vangen's. These scholars sought to examine collaboration generally and across such divergent topical areas as childcare, transportation, environmental issues, health care, education, and economic development in order to offer broadly applicable recommendations. Their underlying premise is that research for social practice should be concerned with the study of general laws as well as the diagnosis of specific situations to connect theory and practice. Huxham and Vangen's approach serves as a guide for this study's design.

Finally, Huxham and Vangen worked to build theory inductively, from naturally occurring data (such as narratives and observations). This study adopts a similar methodological approach in order to apply the theory of collaborative advantage to a sample of long-lasting community collaboratives. The goal of applying this theoretical lens to this sample is to better understand what differentiates partnerships that illustrate collaborative advantage from those that experience collaborative inertia.

2.2 Life Cycle

Organizational life cycle research spans decades (Bonn & Pettigrew, 2009; Downs, 1967; Greiner, 1972; Mintzberg, 1984; Quinn & Cameron, 1983) and provides a framework for understanding how organizations grow and change over time. The life cycle concept captures the transition from organizational birth to maturity to revitalization to decline and death. For this study, life cycle theory captures the underlying theoretical argument: partnerships can grow and change, and adapt or die, over time. Identifying and understanding life cycle stages matters in terms of setting priorities and identifying appropriate management strategies for sustainability. Underpinning the life cycle theory is an evolutionary perspective in which organizations are expected to pass through stages of development (Lester, Parnell, & Carraher, 2003). Overall, growth and development should result in more opportunities and better outcomes.

It is expected that life cycle stages are sequential: the stages can be observed and may be propelled by a sense of crisis (Daft, 2012). Identifying and understanding life cycle stages can provide managers with a "road map" that may help them address issues in a predictable way (Hanks, 1990). Life cycle models typically include three to ten stages and describe a similar pattern of development. The majority of models include variations of a five-stage model. Quinn and

Cameron (1983) detailed the major approaches to categorizing life cycle stages. Despite varied terminology and models, there is a similar structuring of stages across the literature: 1) viability; 2) growth; 3) maturity; 4) revitalization; 5) decline. Each stage presents its own characteristics and problems to solve. Key to identifying and resolving problems at each stage is recognizing changing needs and also adopting adaptive management behaviors (Dodge & Robbins, 1992).

According to Bess (1998), it is assumed that these life cycle stages apply similarly across sectors, although there are few empirical studies to offer confirmation. In 2001, Stevens presented a life cycle model designed specifically for nonprofit organizations. Stevens' model featured seven stages: 1) idea; 2) start-up; 3) growth; 4) maturity; 5) decline; 6) turnaround; 7) terminal. In their study of twelve pioneering human service organizations in California's Bay Area, Kimberlin, Schwartz, and Austin (2011) built upon this work and identified life cycle stages as essential to explaining the long-term viability of nonprofit organizations in their sample. Thus, life cycle theory offers a valuable and appropriate lens to apply to this study.

The life cycle perspective is deeply rooted in the foundations of the natural and social sciences, including biology (O'Rand & Krecker, 1990). The organism metaphor is particularly salient in turbulent environments where flexible approaches are needed for survival (Morgan, 1986). Public and private management scholars have applied this concept to organizational settings to understand "life stages" in a generalized way and provide recommendations for renewal that prevent decline or death. It can be surmised that, just as we have thought about organizations as changing organisms, this lens may also help us understand the ways in which networks can grow and change over time to remain viable (Lowndes & Skelcher, 1998).

2.3 Collaborative Resilience and Adaptive Capacity

Resilience has been defined as the "developable capacity to rebound or bounce back from adversity, conflict, failure, and even positive events, progress, and increased responsibility" (Luthans, 2002, p. 702). Witmer and Mellinger (2016) define organizational resilience as the "ability to adapt to internal/external disturbances, maintain integrity as a system, reorganize itself, and increase capacity by transforming challenges into opportunities for learning and innovation" (pp. 256–257). This study seeks to understand: 1) what are the negative and positive events that require collaborative resilience; and 2) which factors distinguish resilient collaborations over time?

To address these questions, two conceptual frameworks serve as guides. First, Strichman, Bickel, and Marshood's (2008) study of a sample of nonprofit organizations in Israel identified five elements expected to contribute to adaptive capacity: shared vision, inquisitiveness/openness, evaluative thinking/systems thinking, social capital, and external focus/network connectedness (see Table 1). Second, the University of Chicago's National Opinion Research Center's extensive literature review identified seven elements that are expected to contribute to collaborative sustainability over time: leadership, membership diversity, history of collaboration, structure, resource diversity, sustainability plan, and community buy-in (NORC, 2011, pp. 31–34). This study seeks to examine whether these elements help explain the long-term viability of a sample of community collaborations from across the United States.

Table 1 Predictors of adaptive capacity and sustainability

Adaptive Capacity Elements	
Concept	**Description**
Shared Vision	Creating shared understanding, collectively building a shared purpose. Members involved in setting, owning, and implementing a joint vision. Collaborative vision integrated with personal vision. Understanding how job tasks fulfill collaborative goals.
Inquisitiveness/ Openness	Embracing dissent and diversity of perspectives. Willingness to question underlying assumptions and accepted wisdom.
Evaluative Thinking/ Systems Thinking	Understanding interdependence of different parts of collaborative. Recognizing patterns of change/ addressing underlying causes of events/ acknowledging the nature of unpredictability. An "appetite for inquiry": seeking out data and information to learn and then apply and share the knowledge. Data collection, learning, and knowledge development are an essential, collaborative-wide effort. Evaluative activities are considered as a tool for learning and improving performance.
Social Capital	Creating an environment of trust among members. Ensuring that collaborative policies nurture trust. Encouraging of group dialogue, communication, and collective reflection. Signaling the importance

Table 1 (cont.)

Concept	Description
Adaptive Capacity Elements	
	of knowledge sharing and importance of reciprocity. Rewarding collaborative success, not just the individual. Expectation of members to work together. Creating opportunities for interaction (both time and space). Supporting the creation of social networks.
External Focus/ Network Connectedness	Awareness of interdependence with surrounding environment. "Sufficiently porous" to information and ideas and locates resources and capabilities from outside of the collaborative. Understanding potential to create systematic change through strategic alliances and joint efforts. Construction of partnerships or alliances with others. Understanding the needs of collaborative stakeholders.
Predictors of Collaborative Sustainability	
Leadership	Focused and effective leadership; leadership continuity
Membership Diversity	Engaged stakeholders from the community; a variety of sector partners are involved
History of Collaboration	Prior experience working together collaboratively
Structure	Clear operational guidelines; program management policies and procedures; active governing body
Resource Diversity	Political, financial, institutional resources including money, people, goods, and services
Sustainability Plans	Goals and objectives; sustainability strategies; planning and evaluation
Community Buy-In	Community interest and respect for the effort

Source: adapted from Strichman, Bickel, and Marshood, 2008, p. 226; NORC, 2011

3 The Study

The study sample comes from the Foundation Center's Collaboration Hub (formerly the Nonprofit Collaboration Database). The Collaboration Hub is an online repository of collaborations that were considered for the Center's 2009 and 2011 Collaboration Prizes. While the database was initiated to collect nominations for the prize competition, it continues to collect information beyond the prize time frame. To date, it has information on over 600 partnerships from across the United States. The collection represents a valuable source of historical information, as many of the collaborations detailed there have been in existence for years and in some cases decades.

To study elements that help to explain collaborative resilience over time, the sampling frame was limited to voluntary alliances rather than contracted partnerships or mergers. The Collaboration Hub defines alliances as those collaborative arrangements in which "members maintain structural autonomy but have defined roles and responsibilities to achieve specific social goals or purposes." Further, given the study's goals, partnerships including three or more organizations with a history of ten years or more were of special interest for oversampling. In addition, the sampling strategy included the goal of balancing examples of enduring partnerships with those that had ended to provide an opportunity for comparison and contrast.

A sample of sixty-one collaborations was drawn from the Collaboration Hub. Email invitations for phone interviews were sent to the listed contacts from the database, and online searches were conducted in cases of defunct/returned emails. Due to turnover, retirements, dissolution of partnerships, and lack of availability to participate, the final sample consists of nineteen collaborations (31 percent response rate). Of these collaborations, ten remained intact and nine had ended as of the time of the interviews. While seventeen of the nineteen collaborations included three or more partners, it is important to note that two of the examples had just two partners (see Table 2). These were retained in the sample because both Independent Dialysis at Lion's Center and YMCA of Greater Des Moines/Mercy Foundation offered examples of notable partnerships that were no longer active. Also, in both instances, multiple representatives were willing to participate in this study and thus offer a broader view of the collaborative experience.

A total of thirty-five representatives from the nineteen collaborations, including twenty women and fifteen men, were interviewed. One additional interview was conducted with a recommended collaborator, but that individual was not involved with the collaborations in this study. As a result, this thirty-sixth interview is excluded from the analysis. The phone interviews averaged forty-five minutes each. The data collection took place in Fall 2017 and Spring 2018. Most interviewees represent the nonprofit sector (n=30) while the remainder represent government organizations (n=5).

The study sample is geographically diverse: the nineteen collaborations in this study are located in fourteen states. The collaboratives are distributed across the four recognized U.S. Census Bureau Regions: West (including

Table 2 Study sample

Collaboration (*Ended)	Location	Year Established	Number of Partner Organizations
Austin ASPCA Partnership*	TX	2007	5–7
Californians for Pesticide Reform	CA	1997	>10
Care Access for New Americans	MO	2004	8–10
Coordinated Community Response to Domestic Violence	PA	2003	>10
Health Law Partnership	GA	2004	3–4
Independent Dialysis at Lion's Center*	MD	1997	2
Make Medicare Work Coalition	IL	2005	3–4
Mapping Our Voices for Equality*	WA	2010	5–7
Midlands Mentoring Partnership	NE	1999	>10
Nystrom United Revitalization Effort	CA	2002	>10
Pearce Campus Community Resource Center*	IL	2005	>10
Pittsburgh Climate Initiative	PA	2008	5–7
River Region Health Information Organization*	AL	2008	>10
The Homeless Youth System*	OR	1998	5–7
Violence Prevention Coalition	CA	1991	>10
WASH Monitoring Exchange*	VA	2011	5–7
WeGo Together for Kids	IL	2005	>10
Wyoming Community Youth Coalition*	MI	2007	>10
YMCA of Greater Des Moines/ Mercy Foundation*	IA	2008	2

Source: The Foundation Center's Collaboration Hub

California, Oregon, and Washington); Midwest (including Illinois, Iowa, Michigan, Missouri, and Nebraska); South (including Alabama, Georgia, Maryland, Texas, and Virginia); and Northeast (Pennsylvania). The aims of these collaborations are diverse as well. They represent efforts in environmental protection, community education, health promotion, youth development, animal welfare, community development, and human services. However, they are united in the circumstances prompting the collaboration: all of these collaborations report responding to a community need as a catalyst for the effort.

Each interview followed a structured protocol. Interviewees were asked to tell the story of how the collaborative evolved over time, including how the alliance was shaped by individual, collaborative, or systemic factors. Participants were asked to begin with their "origin story" of the collaboration followed by approximately three stories of critical moments that shaped the effort. These moments could be choices, shocks, or opportunities that had a positive or negative effect on the evolution of the collaboration. Interviewees were then asked about the current status of the collaboration, their vision for the future (or legacy, if the collaboration had ended), recommendations for other collaborators working on long-term community issues, and whether they could suggest other partners from the effort who could also speak about the collaboration.

Interviews were recorded and transcribed for analysis. Transcripts were coded using NVivo 11.4.3. The coding process included both interpretive (open) and positivistic (axial) approaches. First, open coding was conducted to identify critical junctures and inductively categorize those junctures into common themes. Second, axial coding matched interview content with concepts from the theoretical frameworks of interest. Matrix coding queries differentiated ongoing and ended collaborations to identify patterns. The qualitative findings were also analyzed descriptively to examine the degree of polyphony (congruence) among collaborators' narratives.

4 Understanding Critical Junctures

Critical juncture analysis is a methodology most readily associated with historical and political studies. However, critical juncture analysis can also be conducted in the context of organizational (or, in this study, collaborative) settings. Identifying critical junctures in the development of an institution can provide a "compelling account" of the mechanisms that gave rise to its legacy (Capoccia, 2015, p. 155). Critical junctures have been defined as "relatively brief periods of momentous political, social, or economic upheaval" (Dion, 2010) when the status quo is challenged and demands for change emerge. However, Capoccia (2015) notes that not all critical junctures necessarily involve significant change: they may instead represent a recommitment to a dedicated course of action. Further, critical junctures can be framed normatively as positive (i.e., successes, opportunities) or negative (i.e., challenges, failures) (Capoccia & Keleman, 2007).

In this study, the goal is to examine the critical junctures that impact collaborative resilience over time. According to Christiansen and Vanhoonacker (2008), the decisions that unfold over time contribute to the "cognitive maps" that create the working theories which in turn impact the actions of the involved individuals. Historical analysis of critical decision points and experiences can help identify those elements that contribute to stability or resilience. According to Bene (2013), there is a need to better understand resilience, and part of this understanding is based on understanding the shocks that require said resilience. To identify and understand those critical junctures, narrative analysis is recommended (Capoccia and Keleman, 2007). For this study, interviewees were asked to tell the stories, or narratives, of the critical moments that impacted their collaboration. A total of 120 critical junctures were reported by 35 participants. The critical junctures were identified and categorized into three categories: systemic, collaborative, and individual. Each category is discussed in the following section, and every effort is made to retain original wording of direct quotes (although names have been removed).

4.1 Systemic

As noted in Section 2 on theoretical foundations, a key goal of this project is to fill the research gap that exists related to understanding the multiple elements of collaboration, including the systemic, collaborative, and individual dynamics that impact the effort. Participants discussed two categories of *systemic* critical junctures: *resources* and *external forces.*

4.1.1 Resources

One of the most notable explanations for the rise of collaborative work is resource dependence theory (Guo & Acar, 2005; Zuckerman & D'Aunno, 1990). Sectors, organizations, and individuals must work together to unite the variety of financial, informational, management, and other resources that are necessary to address a shared problem. The data collected for this research study demonstrates that resource dependence theory is not just an explanation for why collaborations begin. Rather, obtaining, maintaining, or losing resources impacts the long-term viability of a collaborative effort.

One interviewee described the importance of obtaining resources early in the process to build the capacity of the collaborative:

> Well, when we started, it was me part-time, working out of my car with my cell phone, and that was not sustainable. So I think another threshold was [when] we got a first grant from the health foundation that was created in the state of Georgia when our Blue Cross Blue Shield went for profit, and that allowed us to hire an office manager/paralegal and a staff attorney. And then we, a little bit later, applied to the Woodruff Foundation here ... We got a very nice grant from them, which allowed us to hire another staff attorney.

Garnering resources can represent a big win for collaboratives, but the loss of resources can have an equal, opposite effect. An example from an ended partnership illustrates the crush of losing anticipated resources:

> And so we submitted a proposal to the state of Alabama to run the health information exchange for the whole state. If you talk about critical junctures or whatever, this is probably what killed the whole thing, [which] is [that] they gave the contract to someone else. So that kind of put an end to the RHIO, actually.

Given the external and unpredictable nature of resource acquisition and control, collaborative partners must find ways to adapt as they exist within an environment of shifting resources. A third example from an ongoing initiative demonstrates the importance of this ability:

> Not everything goes well. So one I mentioned was the fact that the housing didn't materialize and still hasn't ... And kind of along the way, together with the school district and all these partners, we submitted a grant application for one of the Promise Neighborhoods ... We thought we had all the community partners we needed. We had a good project in front of us, and we were all set to go. And we didn't get funded. And that took a lot of the wind out of our sails, I think, at the time. And we had to rethink how to get things done. And I think it really did set us back in terms of – we had great momentum back then ... But I will say, it didn't cause our partnership to fall apart. It was just sort of, "Okay. We've got to do something different now." But we didn't say, "Okay, I guess we're done," and walk away. We said, "Okay, we've got to adjust." And that was one setback.

4.1.2 External Forces

The previous examples illustrate the value of resource dependency theory in framing systemic critical junctures. In addition to external resources, there are several other systemic forces that represent critical junctures and affect the success of community collaboratives. Crises and economic and policy shifts, as well as windows of opportunity, all serve as key systemic critical junctures for community collaboratives.

The concept of resilience most often applies to acute crises (Quick & Feldman, 2014) which can include both natural disasters or man-made events. One example demonstrates the catalyzing force of a man-made disaster that united collaborative partners to work together in response to a local crisis:

> So another example of kind of a pivotal moment in our collaboration was, well, actually multiple times, whenever there was what we call in our world a man-made disaster. So we respond to hurricanes and tornadoes when animals are in need, but there are often, unfortunately, man-made disasters that are things like hoarding cases or puppy-mill busts or cruelty cases. And there was a terrible hoarding case, and the Humane Society had been called upon to take in, I don't remember exactly, something like 120 of these tiny dogs that had been living in one house, and they were just in absolutely atrocious shape, just really, really – just terrible, I mean, matted fur and feces and sick and all of that kind of stuff. And so they had to bring these animals into their shelter, and we came in and said, "Well, we will do all of the spaying and neutering and vaccinating and just preventative kind of wellness that these animals need," and then our other partner came in and said, "Well, and if any of them test positive for heartworm disease, we'll treat them for heartworms." And so 120 animals would be a heavy lift for one agency, but, between all of us working together, we were able to, in a period of about twenty-four hours – we drove our mobile clinic over to that Humane Society, we got all of the animals spayed and neutered, they were bathed, all their fur had to be clipped off, and they were ready for an adoption so much sooner than they could have been otherwise, which is what we really wanted for them. They'd been through so much; we just did not want them sitting and languishing in the shelter environment. We wanted them in homes. And so that was made possible through that type of partnership, which I thought was a really nice outcome.

Another crisis that impacted community collaboratives broadly was the Great Recession of 2007–2008. In this example, this systemic critical juncture required that the collaborative partners effectively communicate the value of their efforts amid an economic downturn:

> We got tremendous commitment from a number of different organizations from the beginning. They would provide that, but again, as things go on, the economy – about the time we kicked this thing off, the economy tanked. And so that affected a lot of different organizations, but I think people were committed enough to keep it going for a few years simply because we knew that we had made some impact.

Policy changes serve as another external, systemic force that impact community collaboratives. An interviewee from an enduring collaboration addressed one such change and the group's response, which focused on protecting a valuable program:

Well, of course, implementation of Medicare Part D was key, and that sort of doing the education and advocacy and the monitoring of how that was rolling out really lasted for at least, I would say, thirty-six months if not more. But then we faced threats to a program that we created, which is Illinois Cares RX, which was the prescription drug supplemental program we originally created for older adults and people with disabilities who could not afford their drug coverage. And we faced, in starting about 2007, 2008, when state budgets hit an all-time low – we hit that crash. The state eliminated the program, Illinois Cares RX. So it was a critical juncture, because we had to come together, and we had to switch from sort of a monitoring role, and while we had been doing legislative and administrative advocacy just to ensure Medicare Part B was rolled out accurately in the state, we had to get into a defensive posture of defending Illinois Cares RX and trying to protect the program.

An example from an ended collaboration offers an opportunity for comparison. In this case, the obstacles proved too great for the collaboration to overcome in light of the external policy changes:

With the changes in that system, as far as how HIPAA compliance was going, we knew we would have to make a big investment into changing out our software and our hardware for how we were going to utilize the database and have that appropriate system for HIPAA compliance, and there would be no way we could do that. So we began with those three factors, and there's probably others that I'm not aware of, but we couldn't come to any viable solutions as to how we were going to get this operation to operate in the black. Membership wasn't growing, [and we] didn't have the dollars to invest in new HIPAA compliance software. So we began the proceedings to cease the collaborations and began shutting down.

While substantial policy changes can signal the end for some collaboratives, an example from an enduring partnership demonstrates the use of crisis as an opportunity for reframing and resiliency:

So one of the things we did was we said, "Let's convene a big conference, a gang violence prevention and intervention conference, where we can bring everybody together for two days to just be in the same place, and talk, and articulate, and share best practices and what we're doing here, and highlight everybody's work, and start to communicate a story that there doesn't have to be a single model." That even within Los Angeles, what we know is that different things are effective in different regions. So can we start to articulate a collective voice around diverse approaches? And I'll be honest, people were mad at us for doing this because they thought the Violence Prevention Coalition doesn't do gang intervention work, so, sort of, who were we to convene this? And my point was: exactly [laughter]. We don't do it. We're the neutral party. Our entire job is to try to build collective strength and to try to articulate broader strategies, so that's exactly why it should be asked, because it's not one intervention agency trying to bring everybody else together. I have no skin in the game. I don't have an intervention program. I just want to host the conversation so we can, again, start to articulate a collective perspective and to actually say Los Angeles is a place where we should be having this conversation to, sort of, lift that up on a national level.

4.1.3 Lessons on Systemic Critical Junctures

This study reveals two categories of systemic critical junctures: resources and external forces. Two lessons emerge from these findings. First, resource dependence theory is not just an explanation for why collaborations begin. Rather, obtaining, maintaining, or losing resources impacts the long-term viability of a collaborative effort. Second, external events such as crises and economic/policy shifts can disrupt or derail collaborations. On the other hand, such events can strengthen partnerships when they are framed as windows of opportunity.

4.2 Collaborative

To fill the research gap related to understanding the dynamics of collaborative success, this project next considers critical junctures that occur at the level of the collaborative. A variety of critical junctures were identified by the respondents, including aligning mission/purpose, structural investments and changes, as well as both progress and setbacks that impact the internal workings of the collaborative along the way.

4.2.1 Mission/Purpose

The need to align goals and identify common purpose among collaborative partners is one that is echoed by interviewees. For example, one interviewee noted that, in the beginning of the effort, the partners did not have a clear goal, and it was a critical moment when they asked: "What are we trying to achieve together, and how do we work more strategically toward that?" Another described a purpose-finding journey in which partners realized that they first need to learn about one another: "So I think the big thing we had to do on both ends was eat some humble pie and be open to what the hospital needs were, and the hospital needed to be open to what our needs were and what we were trying to accomplish. So that's really – the whole [thing is] seeking to understand the point of view from both organizations." Boundary-spanning alignment of purpose and mission can be aided by the introduction of management tools such as logic models, and this can be a pivotal moment for the group. This collaborator explains:

But over time, we realized, if we really wanted to move the needle for animal care, we really wanted to, say, get the live release rate up at the city shelter, we wanted to reduce the number of animals becoming homeless, reduce the number of animals suffering, and that kind of thing, that we would have to get a lot more strategic. And so, at that time we really set out saying, "Okay, what if we used a logic model [inaudible] and created a comprehensive, community-level strategic plan?" And that, I think, truly was a major game changer, because before that each agency had their own strategic plan, and we were doing a better job of communicating, but we were all kind of working on our own thing.

While the introduction of logic models and planning tools can represent a key development in the history of a collaborative, the accompanying shift in perspective from individual organizations to a collective also represents a critical juncture for partners. A collaborator shared their experience:

Oh, yeah. I mean, well, the logic models we created on our own before the consultant, but the consultant then came in – of course, we shared everything we had done. But they did a strategic plan. That was totally critical to [inaudible] in all of this because what they were able to do is gather a wide stakeholder input and feedback and even have focus groups with survivors and get their input into it. And out of it, the city was involved and in agreement. So it was a shared plan then. It wasn't Women Against Abuse's plan: it was everyone's plan, and that was really important. It's not going to work for us to go deliver a set of goals to somebody and say, "You need to do it," but [it works to] have them share in developing it and doing it together.

4.2.2 Structure

In addition to finding common mission and purpose, ensuring that the right people are involved is an important moment in a community partnership's development. As one collaborator explains, this is a critical juncture in the life of a collaborative:

Getting the meeting to happen was critical groundwork, getting all the right people to the table. So those initial conversations that had to be had – saying, "Hey, we have this idea; we'd all like to come together; we'd like this to be the focus" – getting everyone to be open was – those were critical hurdles and groundwork. So just getting people to the table was – there were hurdles to overcome. So that was the groundwork. And then getting people bought in, like, "Yes, I'm here, but I'm not committed to working with you. What are we talking about?" [Laughter.] More hurdles ... Just getting everybody invested, I would say, is probably the groundwork, the most critical piece of the groundwork.

The ways in which collaborators achieve the goal of having the right people at the table differs considerably. This example illustrates how a collaboration identified key partners and extended an invitation for their participation as part of an advisory board:

> I thought was incredibly important to do was to establish an advisory board for the health-law partnership as a whole. And so I invited a bunch of lawyers that I knew across the town – they tend to be health lawyers – to be an advisory board, again, to build relationship[s], potentially to build a funding stream for other initiatives that the partnership might go on, but also to provide expertise in terms of how to get publicity for the partnership, how to get maybe young lawyers to work in the partnership for a while. That is, continuing to build relationships and establishing a solid foundation within the Atlanta community. I mean, that became also important in laying the foundations.

Bringing in new members can reshape the structure of the initiative. In this case, a partner describes how adding government representatives changed the leadership dynamic within the collaboration over time:

> And we sat down over a series of meetings, said, "So what are we interested in here? What came out of the plan that the residents are interested in, and what are the options?" We quickly brought in the city government and the city manager. In particular, the city of Richmond, who became over time a very key player. So it was initially started without the local government, but, because of good leadership at the city, they became one of the key leaders.

Identifying and adding partners who can lend credibility and expertise is a key need for community collaborations. An opportunity to bring in "champions" for the effort represents a critical juncture:

> But basically it was to get Children's to commit a doctor to be responsible for the project. And that either gave it credibility, or it had credibility and they gave it to – I don't know, again, which is which. But having somebody from the hospital who was the physician champion was a critical thing to do.

Also, it is essential to delegate responsibilities to set a course for the future. Developing "organizational charts," identifying roles, and taking initiative represent some of the most notable critical junctures at the collaborative level. These steps serve to transform the effort from the idea stage to actionable items. As one collaborator explains:

> And I think that if you're looking for a critical moment, that, to me, was a critical moment. It was to take this set of ideas that were all very good ideas and actually put together this organization chart with somebody in charge, and name people on the committees and roles and responsibilities, so that it took it from this sort of neat idea stage about revitalizing the community ... But we turned it, at that point, into a project. And I think that was a critical moment.

Finding ways for all of the partners to contribute to the effort is critical as well. One collaborator described a process in which each had distinct roles that contributed to a kind of synergy in which more could be accomplished together: "we predominantly took the lead on administrative and legislative advocacy, and they took the lead on individual advocacy, and together we did a significant amount of education and outreach." To make this work, partners need to know what they can do to contribute to the effort. In this example, a collaborator described a key moment when a partner offered to step into a leadership role within the group:

> It was the easiest thing just to say, "Pennsylvania Environmental Council, hook, line, and sinker, the new convener of the District Climate Initiative." But the city, at the time, said, "You know what? We're not actually comfortable with that. We want a role. We want to be a co-chair of it or a co-convener." And so that was actually the first time that the city itself had stood up or raised their hand and been like, "We want," not just a voice. Obviously, they drive a lot of things. But, "We want to be responsible." And I think that sense of responsibility we have only seen grow over the past five years in a good way.

Once the right people are in place and roles/responsibilities are assigned, changes to the structure can impact the collaborative's trajectory. One collaborator described change in membership as a critical juncture and considered its impact on the long-term success of the partnership:

> I think keeping the players at the table. One of them moved out of the country ... and I had stayed at ICHS, but we sort of went in [a] different direction with using the stories, and we never really could all give back together with the same kind of energy around sustaining the project. I think that Creative Narrations really tried to for a while, find new partners and new ways to fund it. But they never really could get the right group of people, I think, and support to take it to the next step.

Changes to the collaborative's structure can be especially destabilizing when one of the founders of the effort leaves. In this example, a collaborator described a critical juncture when a key leader moved on and the replacement did not prioritize the collaboration in the same ways as his predecessor:

> Well, another one that shaped the future was when the CEO of the hospital, who was part of the vision of this and could articulate it so well and just saw this tremendous potential in this, left and moved on, moved to another role. And so you get a new CEO in. So, here's your top guy who's the decision maker and who is, I'm not going to say is a new concept, but he didn't come up with the idea and really wasn't quite as – didn't have the same level of passion for the concept that the previous

CEO did. Wasn't necessarily against it, but certainly didn't have the level of passion that the other CEO did. And so then, all of a sudden, it falls down on the priority list, and the involvement, his personal involvement and the involvement of others, declined considerably, and that didn't help. It wasn't necessarily anybody's fault. It's just the way it was, and it just happens as time goes on and you have turnover there.

4.2.3 Progress

Indicators of positive progress toward collaborative goals serve as powerful milestones in the life of a community alliance. In order to effectively gauge progress, however, collaboratives need a plan and actionable steps. Collaborators described critical moments, including their process of identifying how to evaluate success and also moments when they aggressively pursued their goals. They also identified "wins" as critical moments. For example, this collaborator recalled a hard-won legislative victory which was made possible by the collaboration's efforts:

> But at the end of the day, we won, and it was kind of amazing [laughter]. We said, "Whoa." And I think that that early part of the resilience of a group of people that was committed to do a statewide initiative. Which is really, one, a very different thing from doing legislation and a very different thing from doing grassroots organizing, etc., was really an act of resilience and coopera- tion that – I guess I expected it, but it was really a great thing to see happen because people worked together in their special areas extremely well, and we put together a good bill, we found a great sponsor, and we lobbied it every point along the way, and we won.

Progress made in spite of challenging circumstances stands out as a defining moment as well. In this example, a collaborator describes how the group adapted when their long-term goals were not easily or quickly achieved. To maintain community support and momentum, they identified ways to achieve some "small wins" along the way:

> I think as time progressed and as neighbors got disillusioned about how long things took, we had to shift gears a little bit and start doing some immediate, on-the-ground things to keep the residents engaged. So we began investing in some real simple projects like coordinated annual events in the neighborhood. Clean-up days, community garden days, we rebuilt the – in the old Nystrom school building, before the school was finished a year and a half ago, we rebuilt their computer lab. So we did some tangibles that were beyond the regular scope of the five capital projects to really just keep people engaged and to keep the eye on the prize, to use that expression. That bigger goal is taking a long time – we know that – and we have to keep moving.

Adapting to achieve progress is an experience shared by other collaborators as well. In one case, a collaborator noted that their goals weren't working as expected. As a group, they had to reevaluate and make changes. They achieved this by staying "pretty fluid to address what the needs are and what the right thing is to be doing." While they assessed this need for adaption internally, sometimes internal changes emerge from external feedback. In this example, a collaborator describes an example of hard-won progress in which the collaborators successfully won over their opponents:

> Another key moment was probably after this really bad meeting in Stockholm where everyone basically was, "We hate you and your idea." One of those local groups there, I had a follow-up call with them ... and was able to explain the idea a little bit more. And they expressed that they were keen to ... come be a part of this work, and that was definitely kind of foundational moment too, that we kind of won over one of the more opposed groups and then managed to convey a vision that they were also excited about.

Making progress can be a difficult process and the difficulty can be most memorable for partners. In this example, a collaborator describes a challenging experience that pushed the collaborative's progress in some unexpected ways:

> So we went to the WASH – Water and Health Conference at UNC – ... and we put up the indicators, and the room – it was very controversial – the room kind of erupted with, "How can you tell us what to measure?" And, "This is not going to work." And, "It should be governments measuring things." And, "How does this line up with the Joint Monitoring Program?" which is the group that was measuring, at that point, the MDGs, Millennium Development Goals. And it just kind of fell flat. But what was interesting is I think it was good criticism, and it's kind of like, "What is the point of this? Who is the audience?"

4.2.4 Lessons on Collaborative Critical Junctures

This study reveals three categories of collaborative critical junctures: mission/purpose, structure, and progress. Each has the potential to positively or negatively shape the future of the partnership. In terms of mission and purpose, collaborators recall critical moments including the introduction of tools such as logic models to help align their goals. Structural changes, including bringing in new partners or losing committed ones, can substantially change the internal dynamic of the group. Finally, assessing progress, adapting as needed, and using difficult moments as learning opportunities are all illustrations of critical moments that influence the collaboration's trajectory.

4.3 Individual

To address the final element of collaboration, the individual, this section summarizes critical junctures that emerge at this level. Critical junctures can be either positive or negative in nature.

On the positive side, collaborators discuss feeling welcomed and knowing that they can trust others as examples of critical junctures. In one example, a collaborator described a close relationship with a partner from another organization based on their shared areas of expertise and their complementary training backgrounds. Their relationship was described as "good" and "trusting," and it was seen as a benefit to the collaboration. In another example, a collaborator described a relationship in which partners effectively recognized their own individual core competencies as well as the competencies of their partners, which were together necessary to achieve shared goals.

By contrast, there are also examples of negative critical junctures at the individual level. In one example, deep conflict among partners forced one collaborator to issue an ultimatum:

> They didn't buy into it at all. So they sabotaged it at every corner. Even though the board president's a part of it, the administration just [bided] their time because they knew that board presidents come and go. And so it ended up fizzling to the point where I met with the superintendent of the school and I told her, "Look, either we need to be on the same team or I give up."

In another negative example, an interviewee describes a turf battle. However, this example also illustrates how partners can reframe conflict as an opportunity to better understand the needs and objectives of others to improve the overall collaborative effort:

> So I think, in the beginning, everyone's knee jerk reaction was turf battle. Everyone said, "Hey, we do this and we're the data people." And I think on my side it was the matter of figuring out are there really turf battles here? I kind of determined that there weren't, but it was fundamentally different, but it meant a couple things. It meant how you bring those people in in a way that kind of respects their role but also differentiates . . . So there's no way we could make progress without them. We needed them on board, so the question just became, "How do we frame what we're trying to do in a way that excites them, doesn't step on their toes, but kind of draws a clear and necessary role so they can feel that they are a necessary part of it, but it's something different? And how can we show how it brings value to them?" And so I think this took . . . them getting to chill out and think about it a little bit more, but I think, on our side, really figuring out, "How do we describe this in a way that's exciting to them and not scary or threatening?"

4.3.1 Lessons on Individual Critical Junctures

Individual-level critical junctures illustrate both the best and worst of working with other people. Positive, trusting relationships can benefit the collaboration in meaningful ways. Negative interactions, including examples of sabotage and turf battles, can be destabilizing to the effort unless used to reframe conflict as an opportunity for learning and growth.

5 Exploring the Keys to Resilience

Given the theoretical foundations upon which this study is based, and the study's specific goal of testing the theory of adaptive capacity, the data analysis revealed that one expected element of adaptive capacity (see Strichman, Bickel, & Marshood, 2008) was found to distinguish resilient collaborations: *strong social capital*. Specifically, there are three times more mentions of social capital among resilient partnerships than among those that have ended (see Table 3).

Further, four of the seven predictors of collaborative sustainability (see NORC, 2011) were found to distinguish resilient collaborations in this sample: *buy-in*, *leadership*, *structure*, and *resource diversity*. These four predictors are evident more than twice as often among resilient collaborations as compared to those that have ended (see Table 4).

Table 3 Adaptive Capacity Elements

	Inquisitiveness/ Openness	External Focus/ Network Connectedness	Social Capital	Evaluative Thinking/ Systems Thinking	Shared Vision
Resilient	5	17	16	23	16
Ended	6	20	5	20	11

Source: Strichman, Bickel, and Marshood, 2008

Table 4 Predictors of Collaborative Sustainability

	Buy In	History of Collab.	Leadership	Member Diversity	Resource Diversity	Structure	Sustainable Plan
Resilient	22	5	22	6	12	20	12
Ended	10	4	11	7	4	6	15

Source: NORC, 2011

Each of these distinguishing elements will now be elaborated upon with illustrative quotes to explore and explain collaborative resilience as a function of adaptive capacity.

5.1 Social Capital

Strichman, Bickel, and Marshood (2008) describe social capital as an effort to cultivate an environment of trust among members and to ensure that policies build trust. In the following examples, two collaborators describe why this element of adaptive capacity is so important:

> I know these people. I trust them. We've done X, Y, and Z together. This is where we could take it and this is the impact it could have. And if you do that without having a relationship in place, I think it's much harder.
>
> But really, the timing was propelled because I wanted to develop the relationships, because if I didn't develop those relationships this wasn't going to happen. The collaboration wasn't going to happen. I mean, these collaborations absolutely depend on the trust and goodwill that the partners have for each other, and those simply take time. And particularly, they take time when the partners are not historically perceived ... as allies or partners.

Social capital also includes encouraging group dialogue, collective reflection, and other investments in communication. This collaborator described her process for investing in communication and its impact on the work:

> Well, for me, everything is relationship. Everything. And so any time I have a meeting, right, before I know somebody, I meet [them] in a coffee shop. And I get to know them first, so then, every time we meet in the future, it's about work but I really care about you too. And I find that that has been one of the key differentiators in the work that we get to do.

Knowledge sharing and reciprocity can also be illustrations of social capital, as can creating opportunities for interaction. These can lead to long-term relationships that extend beyond the boundaries of the collaboration as described by this collaborator:

> But some of it's just proximity. I mean, it's somebody that you don't know, and suddenly now you're in their walls and you're thinking about problems from their perspective, and you're face to face with another human being. You kind of can't judge them as harshly as maybe you once did. I don't know – I mean, that's interesting. I mean, I would tell you, by the end of it, I would consider these people, I still do, very, very dear friends of mine. I care about these people as individuals and in their lives.

5.2 Community Buy-In

Community buy-in includes community interest and respect for the effort. The data from this sample shows that broader support for the effort serves as a predictor of collaborative resilience. In one example, a collaborator described an effort to turn the tide on gang activity in Wyoming. The partners participated in evening events at schools and churches, and "thousands" of parents and children attended to rally the effort and support the restoration of the community. In another example of community revitalization, the partners incorporated local residents in planning activities for a new community park. In this instance, "hundreds" of people were involved in such design decisions as lighting and fencing choices as well as determining security features of the park.

Working with the community is a critical predictor of collaborative success, but it requires careful planning to be done effectively. For example, one collaborator recalled identifying which communities needed to be involved and how best to engage with members:

> Now part of why we were looking to engage faith communities, particularly in African American communities, particularly in Latino communities, [was] to say, "How do we bring in the voices of the most directly impacted? How do we talk about this in the communities in a way that's going to resonate?"

One of the reasons that community buy-in is so important to collaborative resilience is that it broadens the frame of engagement and widens the ownership of the collaborative's goals. In this example, a collaborator describes how community buy-in is a long-term priority:

> So again, the theme is yes, we're champions, and it's our issue, but the point was it's really everyone's issue. And it's such a huge problem that, if the city doesn't own it as their own issue, we'll never be able to move the needle. And so now the city is taking it up and it's pretty amazing to watch the change that's happening. But you have to be in this for the long haul. If you think this is going to be an initiative and you're done, that is incorrect. This is a permanent change. So we want to go down deep with data fields in the whole city, reporting, and structures, so that people can take it up permanently.

5.3 Leadership

Focused, effective, and continued leadership is another important predictor of collaborative resilience. One of the ways that this element can support collaborative resilience is when there is consistent, long-term leadership in place to guide the effort. As one collaborator described, their collaboration worked well over time because the same three organizations remained as lead supporters of the effort. Further, leaders are important for championing the effort externally and supporting those who are doing the work. One collaborator explains:

> As an example, the chief medical officer. He knows it's important, and while I've been kind of on the ground, doing the work, he understands and supports me in doing that. He provides a buffer and/or the rah-rah at the C-suite level to say, "This is a good thing. They need to keep going. We need to make sure that we can move this forward."

Collaborative leadership differs in considerable ways from leadership within hierarchical organizational settings (Linden, 2010). Rather than working through command-and-control structures and utilizing positional or reward power to achieve goals, collaborative leaders must move the effort in other ways. This example illustrates the distinctive nature of collaborative leadership and how such leaders contribute to the long-term viability of a collaborative effort:

> I've done everything from helping to oversee their research on what people are currently collecting to convening the working groups to developing the standard to developing a repository to – yeah, kind of all the bits and pieces. So I guess I would say I've been the shepherd. I certainly haven't done all of it. Lots of amazing people have put in different pieces throughout the way, and ... I've been coordinating all those bits and pieces throughout the life of the program.

5.4 Structure

Clear guidelines, management policies, and procedures, as well as an active governing body, are all structural elements that contribute to collaborative sustainability over time. In this study, a recurring illustration of structure was the adoption of regular collaborative meetings and goals with timetables. In one collaboration, the group convened every quarter and collectively pursued agenda items that they set at the start of the year. This approach has continued for over fourteen years.

In another instance, a collaborator said that their partnership had regular meetings the first Thursday of each month from 9 a.m. to 11 a.m. for at least ten years. Up to fifty people would attend what became "sacred" meetings. When an idea was floated to discontinue the meetings, the participants strongly objected, saying: "Don't change it. This is how we get our shared professional development. We are able to get to know each other. We're able to work together and problem-solve when we have issues."

As another collaborator explained, an investment in structure really translates into effective management of the goals that the collaboration seeks to achieve:

We do what we say we're going to do, and we're good at ensuring that we take steps in between our coordinating council meetings, so that we're really prepared and people don't feel like they're wasting their time, and [so] that there's a clear role for what they can do and all of that. That's so important too – just good management of the goal.

5.5 Resource Diversity

Diverse sources of support – including a variety of political, financial, and institutional resources such as money, people, goods, and services – is another important predictor of long-term viability, and this study supports that link.

Collaborators discussed the importance of "cobbling" resources together from multiple sources to achieve their long-term ambitious goals. In one instance, a collaboration pursued the goal of building a community childcare center. This required funding from the city, grant funds, and historic tax credits – among other resources – to make this vision a reality.

Another collaborator described the challenging "juggling act" involved in securing and maintaining multiyear funding commitments for multiyear projects. Given the uncertainty of grant funding in particular, collaborators in this study stressed the importance of innovating and diversifying their resource base. As one collaborator explained, recognizing funding trends is a first step to making necessary changes for enhanced collaborative sustainability:

> And I think all three of the respective organizations are saying to ourselves, "The era of just counting on state dollars and philanthropy to sustain just isn't the model that works. Each one of our organizations is looking for ways to tap into training opportunities or fee-for-service type opportunities for funding ... So as a coalition, now, we're sitting around and we're saying, "Okay, well, what would this look like? We have all this training that we've all done. We all have materials that we've developed as part of this coalition. In theory, some of this material could have some value when each one of us goes out and talks to groups. How do we find opportunities for funding out there in the marketplace with these materials, recognizing that these are materials that were built as part of a coalition?"

6 Learning from Failure

As discussed in Section 2 on theoretical foundations, this study is designed to address gaps in the literature and provide tests of such theoretical concepts as collaborative advantage and collaborative inertia (Huxham & Vangen, 2005). Collaborative inertia, or the failure to achieve collaborative goals, can be a powerful mechanism for learning, and there can even be cases of "successful failures" (Edmondson, 2011). The collaborators in this study, regardless of whether their partnerships remained intact or ended, experienced degrees of both success and failure. The qualitative interview data was analyzed to categorize the sources of failure. Given the purposes of this study, the elements presented in this section elaborate the concept of *collaborative inertia* in practice.

6.1 Stress

According to these interviewees, the most frequently cited cause for collaborative failure is stress. There are fourteen references to the connection between such factors as exhaustion, turmoil, and in-fighting and collaborative failure. As one collaborator explained, there was considerable frustration with the collaboration: they saw no way to overcome the circumstances that stood in the way of their success. They decided to discontinue their efforts. Another interviewee described a situation in which partners determined that the collaborative experience required too much time and energy to be worth the effort, in large part due to fighting among the members of the group. In cases in which stress ends the collaboration, it is actually possible to have a happy ending, as this collaborator explains:

> But at the end, there was so much stress and turmoil that I think everyone was just happy to say, "Hey, that was good while it lasted and we need to part ways and move on." Though, by that point, all the players had changed that had originally been at the table, and the understanding of the whole concept of why this was created, that was not in anyone's radar as to how we could operate together.

6.2 Internal Changes

The second most common cause of failure is related to internal change within the collaboration. Collaborators offered examples such as turnover and changing priorities. A variety of "losses" are also cited, including loss of direction, loss of momentum, or loss of the "glue" holding the group together. As one collaborator noticed in hindsight, it was difficult to predict the impact of change on the viability of the collaboration:

> Yeah, it just took constant effort, and, again, my reflection is we didn't put enough effort into that, because once we had built a nice relationship with the leaders that were there, you just kind of feel comfortable. And then when the change takes place, I underestimated the impact of those relationship changes.

6.3 Resources

Resource problems are cited as the third most common cause of failure. The loss of grant funding, operating at a loss, and external impacts such as the Great

Recession of 2008 all factor into discussions of failure. As one collaborator explained, partners must decide how to allocate their limited time and energies, and resources can matter greatly when making those decisions. However, having resources does not always guarantee success, and a lack of resources does not always guarantee failure:

> We've been members of many, many collaborative projects, and my observation has been that nonprofits are often struggling with resources and it is frequently [true] that CEOs volunteer extra time, which they never have, to sit in on meetings and collaborate. And there comes a time when you have to choose, and you must choose those activities that are funded and those activities that are streamlined into helping the agency – and, frankly, paying for your salary. So when collaboratives do include incentives, right, it is my observation that they continue and they then go on to be more successful. [But] not always – it has to do with everybody's willingness to work together regardless of resources, because some collaboratives have been awesome and with no money attached. And some, even despite the resources, have been just a struggle.

6.4 Natural Causes

Some interviewees discussed stages of natural collaborative decline. This shared observation aligns with the life cycle theory of collaborative development, which serves as a theoretical foundation for this work. As one collaborator explained, there was a time period in which the partnership grew to meet an emergent community challenge. As the issue began to diminish, so too did the partnership:

> Well, you know, I've been involved in a lot of different programs in my career, and I think they all have a life … You know, you can go into a nice neighborhood where there's no problems and beat the drum about neighborhood watch and importance of neighborhood watch programs, and neighbors watching out for each other, taking care of each other, and it won't go anywhere until somebody's house gets broken into. And then all of a sudden you got that impetus to say, "Okay. We've got to do something now because something bad happened." And so I think what we saw was an evolution here of some of the more visible indicators and some of the things going on. Graffiti on the street, we had a very aggressive graffiti abatement program. Gang-related crimes, we saw and again that can be a lot of different factors. The gang activities were somewhat diminishing over a period of time. Stuff was happening around the country for the most part, and not necessarily all parts of the country, but in communities like this it's a passing kind of a fad, if you will, that sometimes has a life. But the thing that was driving it at the beginning, that very visible symbol of youth violence in our community, seemed over a period of time to begin to diminish.

One of the most intriguing findings from this study is that life cycle theory, which typically includes a final stage of decline or death, is not a fit for this sample. Instead, the relationships fostered in community collaborative experiences continue on through formal or informal efforts or spin-off projects. There is evidence of a *phoenix effect*: the collaborations that ended did not die in the biological sense, which we would consider to be final and irreversible. Rather, this study reveals that long-term collaborations have a tendency to rise again in unexpected ways, emerging from an end that is rarely permanent.

For example, the Wyoming (MI) Community Youth Coalition, which was a partnership led by the Wyoming Police to address gang prevention, is no longer in its original form due to funding issues and competing priorities. However, part of this effort continues through the OneWyoming cross-sector initiative, which focuses on providing services to families, employment support, poverty reduction, and youth mentoring. Similarly, the Mapping Our Voices for Equality collaboration no longer exists to offer digital storytelling for health outreach and education, but the spirit of the initiative lives on through continued relationships among the collaborators. An interviewee elaborated: "Although I do want to make clear that you're asking about a very specific project, and I would actually say that the group of people that worked on that project, our history of collaboration and relationship-building, to me, is much bigger than Mapping Our Voices. So I think that's a snapshot of a period in time and how our collaboration worked, but I think how those community health schemes worked together over a longer period is kind of the bigger, more long-lasting collaborative piece."

Similarly, the WASH Monitoring Exchange lives on in part through the Water Point Data Exchange, which represents an expansion of that effort. When the River Region Health Information Organization was disbanded due to funding issues, the local parallel efforts, Envision 2020 and the Wellness Coalition, continue today. Further, when the Independent Dialysis at Lion's Center collaboration ended due to changing fiscal and regulatory realities, the positive "win-win" experience meant that collaborators expressed a commitment to working together again should the opportunity present itself: "In fact, I think the last meeting that [we] had, we ended on, "Circumstances change. We would be very, very happy to work with you again." And I think both sides felt that exact same way. And again, with the collaboration itself, it was very successful, in my opinion, and we would be honored to work with them again because they had the same mindset that we did: you put your patients first, and you try to improve their overall quality of life."

7 Resilience and Failure through the Lens of Polyphony

As discussed, this research seeks to examine collaborative resilience using a long-term focus, at multiple levels, and through the experiences of diverse partners to help fill gaps in our shared understanding of this concept. This is achieved by examining the narrative histories of community coalitions with a specific focus on reports of critical junctures that contributed to collaborative advantage or inertia.

According to Capoccia and Kelemen (2007), the perception of critical moments may not be shared by all individuals. When more than one voice is telling the same story, it is said that there is a degree of *narrative polyphony* (Borins, 2011). The alignment in narratives may have implications for problem-framing and problem-solving (Nowell, 2009). It may be expected, for example, that there is more alignment among sustained collaborations and potentially more discordance among those that have ended.

To examine the extent of polyphony, or the similarity among critical junctures reported by the interviewees, four collaborative examples are selected. These examples were selected based on the following criteria: 1) at least three representatives were interviewed from the collaboration to examine a variety of perspectives; and 2) the selection of cases represents an opportunity for comparison and contrast (two of the four examples remain intact and two have ended).

The critical junctures reported by interviewees in the resilient examples represent strong degrees of polyphony (see Tables 5, 6, 7, 8). Example 1 has an agreement rate of 91 percent (eleven of twelve critical junctures are the same), and Example 2 has an agreement rate of 80 percent (twelve of fifteen critical junctures are the same). By contrast, there is less agreement, or polyphony, among ended collaborations. Example 3 has an agreement rate of 66 percent (eight of twelve critical junctures are the same), and Example 4 has an agreement rate of 55 percent (five of nine critical junctures are the same).

These findings offer new insights on understanding why resilient partnerships continue. If collaborators are aligned in terms of their agreement of critical moments, this alignment could be related to alignment in other core collaborative components such as mission, goals, and values, which may in turn improve their chances for success over time. Lack of alignment in narrative accounts of the collaboration's history may signal broader divergence among partners that may impact the long-term viability of the effort.

Table 5 Polyphony Example 1 (Resilient; Discordance Bold)

	Critical Juncture 1	Critical Juncture 2	Critical Juncture 3	Critical Juncture 4
Interview A	New organizational chart identified responsibilities	Funding for major community project initiative	Set-backs: loss of grant and need to demolish community center	N/A
Interview B	Master planning session identified priorities and introduced MOUs	Funding for major community project initiative	Demolition of the community center	N/A
Interview C	Master planning session that focused on vision, quick wins, MOUs	Creative funding for major community project initiatives	Demolition of the community center	**Elected officials adopted a resolution formalizing the collaboration**

Table 6 Polyphony Example 2 (Resilient; Discordance Bold)

	Critical Juncture 1	Critical Juncture 2	Critical Juncture 3	Critical Juncture 4
Interview A	Efforts to involve a key partner were unsuccessful; moved on to another more willing partner	Funding for staff hires and inclusion of a new champion to educate medical partners	Pursuing IRB approval formalized partnership and led to publishing	Creation of evaluation criteria and original database
Interview B	**Bill passed to raise the age for child car seats**	Finding legal-medical common ground by working together	Publishing articles led to greater credibility	
Interview C	Efforts to involve a key partner were unsuccessful; moved on to another more willing partner	**Formalized relationship via joint class**	Pursued IRB for research purposes	Introduction of formal evaluation mechanism

Table 6 (cont.)

	Critical Juncture 1	Critical Juncture 2	Critical Juncture 3	Critical Juncture 4
Interview D	Efforts to involve a key partner were unsuccessful; moved on to another more willing partner	Creation of an advisory board to build relationships; credibility of the new medical partner	**Funding for law school clinic**	N/A

Table 7 Polyphony Example 3 (Ended; Discordance Bold)

	Critical Juncture 1	Critical Juncture 2	Critical Juncture 3	Critical Juncture 4
Interview A	Early structured guidance at meetings	Unclear goals led to need for strategic planning and use of logic models	Coalescing two programs: rabies and spay/neuter clinics	**Addressing a man-made disaster together (animal hoarding)**
Interview B	Team of experts helped guide the collaboration process	**Response to helping animals affected by Hurricane Harvey**	**Faced opposition within the community**	Strategies for working together included focus on reciprocity
Interview C	**Developed shared outcome measures for humane communities**	Use of logic models and data to examine impact over time	Identified ways to fill gaps in service, specifically spay/neuter	Mutual support for one another: attended each other's events

8 Reflections on Success

The community collaborations in this sample all experienced a degree of success, regardless of whether their partnership remained intact at the time of this data collection. When interviewees describe what makes collaboration successful over time, their remarks focus on several key categories. These categories, including relationships, commitment, resources, structure,

Table 8 Polyphony Example 4 (Ended; Discordance Bold)

	Critical Juncture 1	Critical Juncture 2	Critical Juncture 3	Critical Juncture 4
Interview A	Struggled to identify outcome measures	**Unclear who is in charge of the partnership: need to clarify roles**	**Turnover of top leadership**	N/A
Interview B	Advisory committee focused on outcomes measures	**Positive finding that the partnership was reaching more people than expected**	Unequal funding support – had to end because of deficits	N/A
Interview C	Need to reframe outcome measures to focus on quality of life	**Physical therapy and wellness connection**	Partnership dissolved due to financial issues, legal changes	N/A

mission/vision, capacity, and outcomes, help to elaborate what the theory of collaborative advantage looks like in practice.

8.1 Relationships

There are thirty-seven references to the importance of relationships, including the importance of effective communication among partners. The interviewees address the importance of several features of relationships. To begin, they should ideally be respectful, trusting, and be based on equality. One collaborator explained the importance of relationships for collaborative success:

> And I think the other critical piece that occurred was that we made relationship development primary always so that people truly are equals at the table. And I think, in some ways, that was different, because you have agencies who have more power and control, more influence, and we worked hard to make everybody equally welcome and participatory. And we hold that true now, and I hold that up as our number one reason for our success.

Partners should exercise conflict management skills and negotiation skills and invest in their relationships. As one collaborator noted, you either need to have an existing relationship with your partners "or you have to know how to build a relationship." Further, effective communication between partners is illustrated by listening, honesty, and sharing information. Partners are valued for their credibility and integrity. It is also important to compromise when needed.

Lastly, do not underestimate the time required to build relationships. As one collaborator explained, in their context, it took "over a decade," so partners must be willing to put in the necessary time for relationship building. One collaborator summarized the importance of collaborative relationships as follows:

> It just seems like, no matter how you slice it, it all comes down to people. And you can have contracts and you can have written agreements and all that kind of stuff, but it ultimately comes down to people because all of those can be redone. It comes down to people, and so that's it, and that's what we've got to help people learn.

8.2 Commitment

The idea of commitment is reflected as a common theme among interviews. One collaborator said that the key to success is to be "annoyingly persistent" in pursuing goals. Partners should have a long-term perspective and be prepared to work hard to meet their goals. As one collaborator said: "We're not going to flinch when there's a struggle." They should have patience with the present and also hope for the future. Further, they should celebrate success. As one collaborator said, "just celebrating keeping going is important." For another collaborator, persistence was an essential factor for success:

> Well, let me just say that there are two things that I think are critical if you're going to achieve anything, particularly if you're going to achieve things on an interdisciplinary basis. But I think, if you're going to achieve anything, you have to have passion. That's the first thing. I mean, you really have to believe in what it is you want to do and the benefits of that. And you have to be persistent. You can't take no for an answer. You have to be able to deftly change a no into a "Well, not now" or "I don't really have enough information to be able to make a judgement, so I'm going to say no" or "No, maybe at some other time" or "'No' means I need a little more time to think about it." But what happens is, the "no" is a signal that there's something, probably a gap, in the mindset of the other that just needs some time to work with. Because if you're passionate about it, you know it's right. I never, at all, questioned myself as to whether or not this was a worthwhile endeavor. I simply recognized that it was, from everybody's perspective, an unusual thing to do.

8.3 Resources

The theme of resources is represented as often as that of commitment as a key to success. It is important to have sustained investments in the effort. In terms of financial resources, interviewees indicated it may be best to limit the number of funders to a few strong, consistent supporters. Leadership and expertise are equally important resources that are needed continuously. Credit and credibility are also resources that need to be cultivated and managed effectively:

> That's another key, I think, element to a successful partnership ... how are you going to think about ways to foster buy-in from the partners so that everybody's got skin in the game? Everybody gets credit for it. Good to always share the credit.

8.4 Structure

Following resources, structure is the next most prevalent factor for success. Interviewees note the importance of regular meetings, defined roles, mechanisms for transparency and accountability, logic models, non-compete agreements, neutral facilitation, and space for both planning and reflection. Interviews also address the importance of "backbone" supporting organizations that help hold the partnership together over time. A collaborator described what this looks like in practice:

> So I think one thing that made this alliance and made the Make Medicare Work Coalition successful is that one of the lead partners did play that bridge role and sort of a backbone role because we had the policy analysis. We had a bit of the expertise across all of the entities and across all of their constituencies that they served. So we kind of understood where each of them was coming from, and we were able to provide them with timely expertise when needed or we would learn something together. But, in a way, we were able to be that glue that held the collaborative [effort] together. So what it required is that we be a little nimble. So we shifted a little bit, and we made our table bigger, and we brought in these folks who could do more of the on-the-ground legislative advocacy with us as partners.

8.5 Mission/Vision

The "why" of the partnership is critically important to success over time. Partners need to agree on common goals and see the benefits of working together to achieve those goals. They need to believe in the purpose of their efforts and see the big picture or broader imperative for their actions. In one example of a collaborative working on climate change, a representative of the effort said, "The global imperative sure as hell doesn't hurt. Right? I mean, when you have that sort of increasing urgency for climate change around the world, the context for these discussions have just gotten higher stakes globally." Other collaboratives found that the importance of their mission is enhanced when it is connected to broader societal needs and is not seen as a siloed issue:

> And then we had folks who were doing gang intervention and talking about "Here's why gun violence prevention is actually also something you should care about if you care about gang violence prevention." And going down the line, when we were like, "It's not a separate siloed issue," that it tends to get kind of pushed over. It's actually deeply ingrained with all of these other sorts of things and kind of drawing that connection among all of those. So this is actually everybody's issue, and it's not a third rail. It's actually pretty integral to a lot of the prevention strategies and efforts that people are using.

8.6 Capacity

Next, collaborators speak to the importance of sufficient capacity to turn goals into actions and results. Partnerships need capacity to effectively use resources. They need capacity to act on behalf of their represented organizations. They also need the capacity to grow, change, and learn over time. As one collaborator noted, honestly reflecting on available capacity to contribute is a critical factor for collaborative success:

> If we're going to be a partner, then you have to actually be capable of contributing to the project. And we got to the point where, at least, I felt, yes, we can take this on. I felt we would be a good, capable contributor. And it was only after that point that we put ourselves onto the organization chart and said, "This is our role."

8.7 Outcomes

Finally, when collaborators discuss what success looks like, they are surprisingly least likely to focus on outcomes. Given the driving forces of mission, purpose, and goals for community collaborations, it is interesting to note that only five references in this study speak to the connection between collaborative success and outcomes of interest. One illustrative quote supports this point:

> I would be interested in how many other collaborations are based on data. I've been in nonprofit work for thirty years, and I've seen collaborations done –
> I mean, it's important to have agencies talking but it's always – I've seen many examples where it's just collaboration in name only. And I feel like when you have data that it takes it to a different level of, I don't know,

deepness or whatever. Depth. Because there's something real that you're trying to move the bar on . . . It needs to be measurable.

9 The Goal of Resilience: Leaving a Lasting Legacy

This study raised an additional question of interest as it proceeded: *why does resilience matter to collaborators?* Three legacy wishes emerged from the interviews with experienced collaborators. First, the participants in this study want to know that their long-term collaborative efforts made a - difference. Second, they wish for their work to serve as an example for others. Third, they want to be able to learn for the future. Each of these legacy wishes is elaborated in the following sections, along with illustrative examples from a variety of community collaboratives.

9.1 To Know We Made a Difference

The top category of legacy wishes focus on outcomes. Specifically, interviewees focused on the legacy of making a contribution or solving a problem. They framed this in ways that matched their collaborative goals: leading the way to a better answer to a problem, helping neighbors, improving lives, getting people onboard with a common goal, helping people work together with others, fostering a larger sense of community, offering good care and services, keeping promises, serving as a catalyst for change, and offering fellowship and joy to people.

> **Collaborative Example 1:** I think one of the lasting hopes is that it really fosters a larger sense of community across a pretty diverse range of organizations that is very – how people think across fields and across sort of different focus areas to try to imagine that as more collective approach to building community health.
> **Collaborative Example 2:** And for so many patients, that absolutely dramatic, and I do mean dramatic, impact on their life and on their quality of life and on their death – we had many that were terminally ill, but those last months of their life, their quality, and them dealing with that was tremendously enhanced by the healthy living center and the bonds that they had created there with other people going through similar stuff that they were and with the staff, very caring staff. And that's something that was – we couldn't have done that by ourselves, and the hospital couldn't have done that by themselves. We could only have done that together.
> **Collaborative Example 3:** And ultimately, the goal is we really are leading the struggle toward ending domestic violence. And when I say it, I believe that we can do it. It's a long-term goal, but we can certainly do it. And we want to figure out how do we align everything to make it happen.

Collaborative Example 4: And I'm hoping that if we can make a difference in one kid's life, it's worth every penny, every hour, that we spend trying to do the things that we're doing.

9.2 To Serve as an Example

The second most frequent legacy wish focused on telling a story that resonates with – and can be replicated by – others. Serving as an example is illustrated in many ways, including through publications and data sharing, being contacted for advice, and also having the collaboration recognized and appreciated for its work.

Collaborative Example 1: We have successfully consulted on the development of a medical-legal partnership in Macon. And so they now have a medical-legal partnership that deals with adults and pediatrics. But it's been because of us going down there and doing lectures and people talking to lawyers and some of our lawyer friends talking to other lawyers that that has been successful. So we now have two medical-legal partnerships in the state, which is great. And I don't think, as long as we're around, we're gonna stop until we get at least one or two more that deal specifically with pediatrics.

Collaborative Example 2: Well, I would like to see that Philadelphia slowly adopts and implements, deep into its infrastructure, the goals of Shared Safety. And then I would also like to document what Shared Safety is, how it came about, etc., so that we can share the model with other cities and hopefully have a broad sweeping change based on our experience here. So I think a lot of it is going to be writing, packaging tool kits and materials, publishing things about the validity of some of the tools, or just the history of coming up with this, what we think were the critical pieces and parts, so that people can replicate it.

Collaborative Example 3: So it would be really great if we had the chance to demonstrate our efforts and our successes. Because this is replicable to other venues. This is replicable to substance abuse. This is replicable to children. This is replicable to providing other services to other cities, whatever. So I think we really succeeded, and I think that we built a very strong partnership.

Collaborative Example 4: The programming was just outstanding. We had people from over fifty cities come in and visit. Hospital, YMCA collaborations from across the country. Had someone from Australia come visit. Had someone from Canada come visit that had heard about it. It was just a tremendous concept, and everybody looked at it, and they said, "This is amazing." When you've got elite athletes – and we had many, many triathletes and marathon runners that were at the elite level – right next to someone who's recovering from cancer, someone who's had a stroke who can hardly walk, I mean, it's just a phenomenal thing to see.

9.3 To Learn for the Future

The third most frequent legacy wish is to learn for the future. Collaborators noted that they hoped that the experience would help them address future challenges and projects, engage new funding streams, or understand problems in a different way.

> **Collaborative Example 1:** Probably first and foremost [is] that it was before its time. That it was a solid idea. It was just before its time, before people really could embrace what collaboration is. Second, that some good things came from it: that it did serve as a catalyst for agencies to bloom for people to help as it moved toward that.
>
> **Collaborative Example 2:** It became real clear that we didn't have a revenue stream that was sustainable, and then so, if you think about it this way, what happened was we really ended up having gotten very focused on "How do we find funding to support what we're doing?" as opposed to "How do we come together to really support our members?" So coming back to our roots is "What do we need to do? What can we do to bring value to our members?"
>
> **Collaborative Example 3:** Because without having people to stand back and really hone in on what's working and what isn't ... my goal is we just shorten the learning curve. We can do things so much quicker if we just learn from each other and just pull it forward.
>
> **Collaborative Example 4:** When I reflect on how long we've been doing it, I think, "Wow, we've accomplished a lot," and then at the same time I think, "Why haven't we accomplished more? Why are we so shortsighted with this or that?" And you can only do so much at a time ... And so it is that's when the patience comes back in and perspective. But so our future is that we're really looking to find ways that we engage some different funding streams to maybe look at policy for the work and doing a better job on communicating the data and the outcomes.

10 Recommendations

This project provided a unique opportunity to ask seasoned collaborators to share their insights for other collaborators who are working on long-term issues in communities across the nation. Their recommendations include focusing on purpose, relationships, structure/governance, and outcomes.

10.1 Focus on the Purpose

The top recommendation is to continually "stay on mission." One collaborator noted: "You have to continually come back to your core purpose for being there and then make sure you still have the right people at the table." It is this "common thread" that must ground all future work of the collaborative, said an interviewee. The following quote summarizes this perspective:

Number one is: why are you collaborating in the first place? If you lose sight of why you've built this collaboration, it's going to fail. It absolutely will fail. It may not fall apart and dissolve, but it'll become ineffective. You'll have a collaboration in name only, and it'll be largely ineffective because you lost sight of why you created the collaboration.

Further, the participants in this study recommend focusing on whom you serve and the greater good and to be persistent in pursuit of goals and avoid losing momentum along the way:

One thing I would say is don't let yourself lose momentum. And we still meet as a group, as I've said, even though there's not a big project still in front of us. But I mean, it's not ready to go. We don't have the housing yet which will drive this, I think. But the fact that we've maintained momentum on this particular effort has allowed these secondary projects and these offshoots to take shape and to continue.

10.2 Focus on Relationships

The second most frequent category of advice centered on relationships. Interviewees focus on managing conflict continuously. They also recommend training and mentoring people on how to collaborate. Also, they suggest focusing on relationships before money, working to understand one another, and not burning bridges. One collaborator elaborated:

Well, I mean, one of the things we've learned over time – I mean, Pittsburgh is a small enough place that you can't burn bridges. Right? So I mean, anybody who wants to spend their career in Pittsburgh sort of knows, whether you agree or don't agree with someone, you kind of have to work together to get to the place where everybody needs to be to take a step forward. So understanding that, and knowing when to back off a little bit and when to push, that's a fine balance that, if you can do it well, helps drive good collaborations.

Another collaborator discussed the importance of investing in effective, and sometimes difficult, communication to avoid misunderstanding and build trust among partners:

I think the big thing is communication, listening, and making sure that you have those open and honest conversations. I mean, if there's something that's working, make sure you praise it. And if there's something that's not working, let your partner know, because a lot of times you come at things from different perspectives and you're only seeing from your perspective. And you have to have that ability to say the hard things and work through them to make it better for everybody. But I do think that communication is the key – I mean, if you can openly discuss what's working, what's not working, and both keep your same intentions of making it successful.

Finally, one interviewee introduced a collaborative relationship "golden rule": be the kind of partner you want others to be.

> And I do think it's important in any type of collaboration to do what you say you're going to do. If you say you're going to do it, do it. Don't waste people's time. As soon as you don't deliver and start wasting people's time, you're losing it. You're going to lose all of it. And when the stakes are so high, we don't have the luxury of acting that way. So I just encourage people to be good and great partners, the way you would want people to be to you.

10.3 Focus on Structure and Governance

Collaborators cite attention to governance and structure as the third most important priority for sustainability. They recommend clarifying roles and responsibilities and making sure the right people are at the table, especially people who will commit to the effort for the long term. The concept of "backbone" organizations emerged again as a critical component for success. As one collaborator noted, such organizations can offer strong project management to keep the partners united and the effort going over time.

The interviewees also recommend engaging in collaborative succession planning, especially related to top leaders. It is also important to ensure an equitable balance of power, engage a neutral mediator, invest in project management, take time for intentional planning, avoid politicizing issues within the group, and ensure that there are processes in place for transparency and accountability, especially when managing funding. One collaborator noted how important ground rules and processes are for making funding decisions and addressing any potential power imbalances. These structures are necessary to avoid conflicts or misunderstandings, especially if the funding is administered by – or serves to benefit – one partner in particular.

10.4 Focus on Outcomes

The least common recommendation from these experienced collaborators is to focus on outcomes. When they do so, the interviewees highlight the importance of setting reasonable expectations. For example, one interviewee noted that partners often "jump into these things, and we want to pitch everything in the first year, and it's just not going to happen." These experienced collaborators remind others that the path to collaborative success may change with time: it is important to be open to those shifts. One collaborator explained this as follows:

> And I think that that's not just true of collaborations, but you kind of develop things as you go along, not because you have this master plan . . . but a lot of it

has to do with you add[ing] pieces as you see the opportunity arises to do that . . . What happened here and what always seems to happen is that you make changes gradually, and things happen. And you work through problems in doing it.

11 Paradoxical Reflections

When examining the categories of recommendations offered to other collaborators (focus on purpose, relationships, structure/governance, and outcomes) there is a stark contrast with the factors for success and failure. Specifically, despite the clear importance of resources in both the success and failure of long-term collaborative efforts, interviewees do not focus on obtaining or retaining resources as a recommendation. A question emerges: do collaborators tend to focus on those elements that are more within their control as opposed to those that may be controlled by external forces?

Further, the most frequently cited source of collaborative failure is stress. It is curious to note that collaborators do not focus on self-care recommendations to help buffer against such stresses as fatigue, excess "busyness," and frustration. Huxham and Vangen (2005) introduced the idea of "partnership fatigue," which is a concept that emerges from these interviews as well. Given the collective focus of collaborative efforts, individual care may be a blind spot for partners. Balancing the need to take care of the group and take care of the individual in these initiatives should be a priority. Just as collaborative scholarship has largely neglected the individual level in empirical studies, this finding suggests that this level may also be neglected in practice as well.

Finally, it is interesting to note that, when asked about their hopes for the legacy of their work, respondents put collaborative outcomes at the top of the list. Interviewees focus on the impact of making a contribution or a difference in their communities, serving as an example to others, or learning for the future. However, in their explanations for success and recommendations for other collaborators, outcomes are mentioned least often. Collaborators may want to believe that investing in relationships and remaining committed to a vision are the most important elements to long-term success, but it may actually be the tangible outcomes that we hold on to most strongly. This suggests an area for future study and theoretical development.

12 Conclusion

As noted by Koliba, Meek, Zia, and Mills (2018), the study of collaboration has evolved over time to include new methods, models, and theories. This study seeks to add to that evolving body of knowledge by examining a sample of community collaborations over time. In summary, several specific contributions of this investigation are worth noting:

1. To address the research gap that exists related to long-term collaborative studies, this project utilizes the *critical junctures methodology* to examine the systemic, collaborative, and individual factors that shape collaborations over time;
2. To address the research gap that exists related to the theoretical and practical understanding of collaborative resilience, this research offers insights into the *features that distinguish resilient collaborations*, including: social capital, community buy-in, leadership, structure, and resource diversity;
3. To address the research gap that exists related to testing existing theories in collaborative settings, the findings provide insights on collaborative failure, including *lack of polyphony* as well as evidence of a *phoenix effect* which suggests the collaborative life cycle rarely includes permanent death; and
4. To address the research gap that exists in terms of multilevel analysis and inclusion of diverse partners, this study offers recommendations for others engaged in the important and challenging work of cross-sector collaboration and also highlights the *dissonance that can exist between individual wishes and collective realities*.

There are several limitations to consider. First, while small sample studies can offer authentic, rich qualitative data, generalizability and replicability is a concern. To this point, capturing a broader sample of representatives from long-term collaborations is challenged by turnover and retirements over time. A second limitation of this work is that interviews were coded by a single coder. Certainly, the presence of an additional coder (or coders) can offer a measure of added reliability. Third, stark distinctions between "resilient" and "ended" collaborations do not tell the whole story. As noted, all of the collaboratives studied for this project illustrate measures of both success and failure. A binary designation, while necessary for comparative purposes, does not capture the nuances presented by the data for this project.

When this study was in its infancy, the envisioned goal was to fill a gap in the literature and answer the following question: *what causes collaborations to fail, and what can we learn from those failures?* However, as this project proceeded, it soon became clear that there was not a single example of failure in this group of collaborations. Rather, in every case, even in those instances when the collaboration ended, there were examples of success: spin-off projects, continued relationships, sharing of lessons learned, and new directions for future initiatives. Community collaboration has a generative power. Further, across all cases, the men and women interviewed for this project expressed an enduring concern for their communities and for their collaborative partners. They shared big dreams for addressing collective problems. They experienced great collective successes in that journey as well as some crushing disappointments. These interviewees described their experiences in ways that helped illustrate both the joys and the challenges of collaborating together over time.

The collaborators interviewed for this project highlighted the importance of starting with the lofty "why" but finishing strong by addressing the enduring, practical elements of collaboration, including "who" and "how." Despite the many challenges that they each faced in their community collaboratives, interviewees considered the hard work of collaboration to be a worthy and gratifying experience: they strongly recommended the tough yet rewarding path for others. One collaborator reflected: "We're patient and tenacious, and we were capable ... That's not to say we didn't take breathers and not to say that we weren't upset by the roadblocks in the way. But I think we're all very glad that we stuck with it." Another said, "Well, I mean, you've really got me thinking and I do thank you for jarring some of those memories, because that was a very, very nice time in my career. It was something that you were proud of. But I would say that collaborations are a necessary part of healthcare. You may not have the specific skill set, but, if you find the right partner that is there to support your services, you can have a very successful collaboration as long as you both go into it for the right reasons."

Hopefully this study sheds light on collaborative resilience for readers from the worlds of both scholarship and practice to guide future efforts. It is expected that collaboration is not a passing fad but rather a requirement for addressing society's most pressing future problems. One interviewee echoed this assessment: "Because I think partnerships and collaborations are going to be the way of the future. It's going to be the only way that I think we're going to be able to make significant impact on our communities and make those changes. And we can't do it alone."

While this study highlights both the great opportunity for and the daunting challenges of community collaboration, the final word for this study comes from an experienced collaborator with advice for anyone considering joining such an effort: "I think it's awesome. Again, I love collaborative work. I had such a good experience with a collaboration personally and professionally that I just would encourage others to take the journey and put themselves into it, because really wonderful things can happen out of it if you make the commitment to put yourself in and do the work and connect with the common thread and keep going. I am a big fan, again, of collaboration, and so I would say, 'Good luck, everyone. Do it.'"

References

Agranoff, R. & McGuire, M. (2004). *Collaborative public management: New strategies for local governments*. Washington, DC: Georgetown University Press.

Bene, C. (2013). Towards a quantifiable measure of resilience. Brighton, UK: Institute of Development Studies.

Bess, G. (1998). A first stage organization life cycle study of six emerging nonprofit organizations in Los Angeles. *Administration in Social Work*, 22 (4), 35–52.

Black, A. & Hughes, P. (2001). *The identification and analysis of indicators of community strength and outcomes*. Canberra: Department of Family and Community Services.

Blackmar, J. M., Getha-Taylor, H., Moen, J. R., & Pierce, J. C. (2018). Connecting Sustainability and Collaboration: Lessons from All America Cities. *National Civic Review*.

Bonn, I. & Pettigrew, A. (2009). Towards a dynamic theory of boards: An organizational life cycle approach. *Journal of Management and Organization*, 15, 2–16.

Borins, S. (2011). *Governing fables: Learning from public sector narratives*. Charlotte, NC: Informatio Age Publishing.

Bryson, J. M. Crosby, B. C., & Stone, M. M. (2015). Designing and implementing cross-sector collaborations: Needed *and* challenging. *Public Administration Review*, 75(5), 647–663.

Bryson, J. M., Crosby, B. C., & Stone, M. M. (2006). The design and implementation of Cross-Sector collaborations: Propositions from the literature. *Public Administration Review*, 66, 44–55.

Butterfoss, F. D. & Kegler, M. C. (2002). Toward a comprehensive understanding of community coalitions. *Emerging theories in health promotion practice and research*, 157–193.

Capoccia, G. (2015). Critical junctures and institutional change. *Advances in comparative-historical analysis*, 147–179.

Capoccia, G. & Kelemen, R. D. (2007). The study of critical junctures: Theory, narrative, and counterfactuals in historical institutionalism. *World Politics*, 59(3), 341–369.

Christiansen, T. & Vanhoonacker, S. (2008). At a critical juncture? Change and continuity in the institutional development of the Council Secretariat. *West European Politics*, 31(4), 751–770.

City of Philadelphia (2019). SMARTCITYPHL Roadmap. Accessed online at: www.phila.gov/media/20190204121858/SmartCityPHL-Roadmap.pdf

Community Tool Box (2018). Chapter 3, Section 5: Analyzing Community Problems. Accessed online at: https://ctb.ku.edu/en/table-of-contents/assessment/assessing-community-needs-and-resources/analyzing-community-problems/main

Cornforth, C., Hayes, J. P., & Vangen, S. (2015). Nonprofit–public collaborations: Understanding governance dynamics. *Nonprofit and Voluntary Sector Quarterly*, 44(4), 775–795.

Daft, R. (2012). *Organization theory and design*. Boston, MA: Cengage.

Dion, M. (2010). *Workers and welfare: Comparative institutional change in twentieth-century Mexico*. Pittsburgh, PA: University of Pittsburgh Press.

Dodge, H. J. & Robbins, J. E. (1992). An empirical investigation of the organizational life cycle model for small business development and survival. *Journal of Small Business Management*, 30(1), 27–37.

Downs, A. (1967). The life cycle of bureaus. In A. Downs, ed., *Inside bureaucracy*. San Francisco, CA: Little, Brown, & Co.

Edmondson, A.C. (2011). Strategies for learning from failure. *Harvard Business Review*.

Emerson, K. & Nabatchi, T. (2015). *Collaborative governance regimes*. Washington, DC: Georgetown University Press.

Forrer, J. J., Kee, J. E., & Boyer, E. (2014). *Governing cross-sector collaboration*. San Francisco, CA: Jossey-Bass.

Gazley, B. & Guo, C. (2017). What do we know about nonprofit collaboration? A comprehensive systematic review of the literature. *Academy of Management Proceedings*.

Greiner, L. (1972). Evolution and revolution as organizations grow. *Harvard Business Review*, 49, 37–46.

Guo, C., & Acar, M. (2005). Understanding collaboration among nonprofit organizations: Combining resource dependency, institutional, and network perspectives. *Nonprofit and Voluntary Sector Quarterly*, 34(3), 340–361.

Hanks, S. H. (1990). The organization life cycle: Integrating content and process. *Journal of Small Business Strategy*, 1(1), 1–13.

Hicklin, A., O'Toole, L. J., Meier, K. J., & Robinson, S. E. (2009). Calming the storms: Collaborative public management, Hurricanes Katrina and Rita, and disaster response. In R. O'Leary & L. B. Bingham, eds., *The Collaborative Public Manager: New Ideas for the Twenty-First Century*. Washington, DC: Georgetown University Press, pp. 95–114.

Hillard Heintze (2018). Championing community policing: Collaboration, change, and a "can-do" attitude. Accessed online at: www.hillardheintze.com/wp-content/uploads/2018/12/Hillard-Heintze-360-Insight-Championing-Community-Policing.pdf.

Huxham, C. & Vangen, S. (2005). *Managing to collaborate: The theory and practice of collaborative advantage.* London: Routledge.

International City and County Management Association (ICMA) (2019). A two-way process: How Aurora, Colorado, serves its immigrant and refugee communities.

Kapucu, N., Hu, Q., & Khosa, S. (2017). The state of network research in public administration. *Administration & Society*, 49(8), 1087–1120.

Keast, R. & Mandell, M. (2014). The collaborative push: Moving beyond rhetoric and gaining evidence. *Journal of Management & Governance*, 18(1), 9–28.

Kettl, D. F. (2002). *The transformation of governance: Public administration for the twenty-first century.* Baltimore, MD: Johns Hopkins University Press.

Kimberlin, S. E., Schwartz, S. L., & Austin, M. J. (2011). Growth and resilience of pioneering nonprofit human service organizations: A cross-case analysis of organizational histories. In M. J. Austin, ed., *Organizational Histories of Nonprofit Human Service Organizations*. London: Routledge, pp. 13–37.

Koliba, C. J., Meek, J. W., Zia, A., & Mills, R. W. (2018). *Governance networks in public administration and public policy.* London: Routledge.

Lester, D. L., Parnell, J. A., & Carraher, S. (2003). Organizational life cycle: A five-stage empirical scale. *The International Journal of Organizational Analysis*, 11(4), 339–354.

Linden, R. M. (2010). *Leading across boundaries: Creating collaborative agencies in a networked world.* Hoboken, NJ: John Wiley & Sons.

Lowndes, V. & Skelcher, C. (1998). The dynamics of multi-organizational partnerships: an analysis of changing modes of governance. *Public Administration*, 76(2), 313–333.

Luthans, F. (2002). The need for and meaning of positive organizational behavior. *Journal of Organizational Behavior: The International Journal of Industrial, Occupational and Organizational Psychology and Behavior*, 23(6), 695–706.

Milward, H. B. and Provan, K. G. (2000). Governing the hollow state. *Journal of Public Administration Research and Theory*, 10(2), 359–379.

Mintzberg, H. (1984). Power and organization life cycles. *Academy of Management Review*, 9(2), 207–224.

Mitchell, G. E., O'Leary, R., & Gerard, C. (2015). Collaboration and performance: Perspectives from public managers and NGO leaders. *Public Performance & Management Review*, 38(4), 684–716.

Morgan, G. (1986). *Images of organization*. Thousand Oaks, CA: Sage.

National League of Cities (2019). How Detroit created a green oasis in the middle of Motor City. Accessed online at: https://citiesspeak.org/2019/01/29/how-detroit-created-a-green-oasis-in-the-middle-of-motor-city/.

NORC (2011). Developing a conceptual framework to assess the sustainability of community coalitions post-federal funding. Accessed online at: https://aspe.hhs.gov/pdf-report/developing-conceptual-framework-assess-sustainability-community-coalitions-post-federal-funding.

Nowell, B. (2009). Out of sync and unaware? Exploring the effects of problem frame alignment and discordance in community collaboratives. *Journal of Public Administration Research and Theory*, 20(1), 91–116.

O'Leary, R. & Vij, N. (2012). Collaborative public management: Where have we been and where are we going? *The American Review of Public Administration*, 42(5), 507–522.

O'Rand, A. M. & Krecker, M. L. (1990). Concepts of the life cycle: Their history, meanings, and uses in the social sciences. *Annual Review of Sociology*, 16, 241–262.

O'Toole, L. J. (2014). Networks and networking: The public administrative agendas. *Public Administration Review*, 75(3), 361–371.

Quick, K. S. & Feldman, M. S. (2014). Boundaries as junctures: Collaborative boundary work for building efficient resilience. *Journal of Public Administration Research and Theory*, 24(3), 673–695.

Quinn, R. & Cameron, K. (1983). Organizational life cycles and shifting criteria of effectiveness: Some preliminary evidence. *Management Science*, 29(1), 33–41.

Stevens, S. K. (2001). *Nonprofit lifecycles: Stage-based wisdom for nonprofit capacity*. Long Lake, MN: Stagewise Enterprises.

Stoker, P., Pivo, G., Howe, C., Elmer, V., Stoicof, A., Kavkewitz, J., & Grigg, N. (2018). Joining-up urban water management with urban planning and design. The Water Research Foundation.

Strichman, N., Bickel, W. E., & Marshood, F. (2008). Adaptive capacity in Israeli social change nonprofits. *Nonprofit and Voluntary Sector Quarterly*, 37(2), 224–248.

Torfing, J. (2016). *Collaborative innovation in the public sector*. Washington, DC: Georgetown University Press.

Witmer, H. & Mellinger, M.S. (2016). Organizational resilience: Nonprofit organizations' response to change. *Work*, 54(2), 255–265).

Zuckerman, H. S. & D'Aunno, T. A. (1990). Hospital alliances: Cooperative strategy in a competitive environment. *Health Care Management Review*, 15(2), 21–30.

Cambridge Elements ≡

Public and Nonprofit Administration

Andrew Whitford
University of Georgia

Andrew Whitford is Alexander M. Crenshaw Professor of Public Policy in the School of Public and International Affairs at the University of Georgia. His research centers on strategy and innovation in public policy and organization studies.

Robert Christensen
Brigham Young University

Robert Christensen is professor and George Romney Research Fellow in the Marriott School at Brigham Young University. His research focuses on prosocial and antisocial behaviors and attitudes in public and nonprofit organizations.

About the Series

The foundation of this series are cutting-edge contributions on emerging topics and definitive reviews of keystone topics in public and nonprofit administration, especially those that lack longer treatment in textbook or other formats. Among keystone topics of interest for scholars and practitioners of public and nonprofit administration, it covers public management, public budgeting and finance, nonprofit studies, and the interstitial space between the public and nonprofit sectors, along with theoretical and methodological contributions, including quantitative, qualitative and mixed-methods pieces.

The Public Management Research Association

The Public Management Research Association improves public governance by advancing research on public organizations, strengthening links among interdisciplinary scholars, and furthering professional and academic opportunities in public management.

Cambridge Elements ≡

Public and Nonprofit Administration

Elements in the Series

Motivating Public Employees
Marc Esteve and Christian Schuster

Organizational Obliviousness: Entrenched Resistance to Gender Integration in the Military
Alesha Doan and Shannon Portillo

Partnerships that Last: Identifying the Keys to Resilient Collaboration
Heather Getha-Taylor

A full series listing is available at: www.cambridge.org/EPNP